Patterns of Light

Rebecca E Nelson

&

Catherine Chandler

Becky Nelson

Published by Leador Publications

Ovel-Tyne, Fuller Street, Nr Fairstead, Chelmsford, Essex, CM3 2AY

Email: admn@leadorpublications.com

Printed and bound in Great Britain

A catalogue record for this book is available from the British Library

www.leadorpublications.com

www.patterns-of-light.co.uk

ISBN: 978-0-9558419-0-3   ISMN: 979-09002148-0-5

Patterns of Light

Verse and illustration

Rebecca E Nelson

Music

Catherine Chandler

for my beautiful grandchildren, Kieran, Cailyn and Erin and all my grandchildren yet to be, with love

Patterns of Light

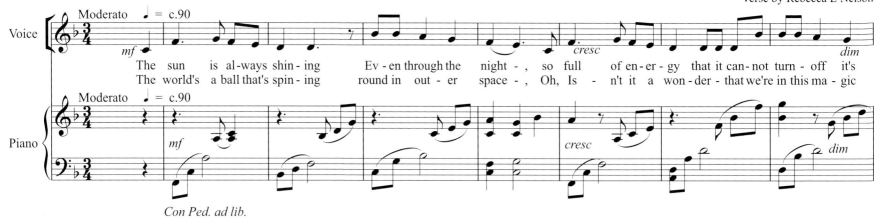

Music by Catherine Chandler
Verse by Rebecca E Nelson

The sun   is al-ways shin - ing   Ev - en through the   night -, so full   of en-er - gy that it can-not turn - off   it's
The world's   a ball that's spin - ing   round in out - er   space -, Oh, Is - n't it a won-der - that we're in this ma - gic

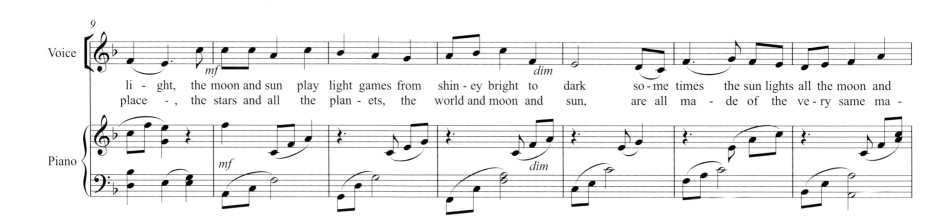

li - ght, the moon and sun   play light games from   shin - ey bright to   dark   so - me times   the sun lights all the moon and
place -,   the stars and all   the plan - ets, the   world and moon and   sun,   are all ma - de of the ve - ry same ma -

ISMN: 979-09002148-0-5

For Hannah

The sun is always shining
Even through the night.
So full of energy that it
Cannot turn off its light.

The moon and sun play
light games
From shiney bright to dark.
Sometimes the sun lights
all the moon
And sometimes only part.

The stars they do a-twinkle
Just for me and you.
And, though you won't believe it,
They are there in daytime too.

The world's a ball that's spinning
Round in outer space.
Oh, isn't it a wonder
That we're in this magic place.

The stars and all the planets,
The world and moon and sun,
Are all made of the very same
Materials re-spun.

Outer space is massive,
Some say infinity,
Much bigger than our
minds can think.
This only God can see.

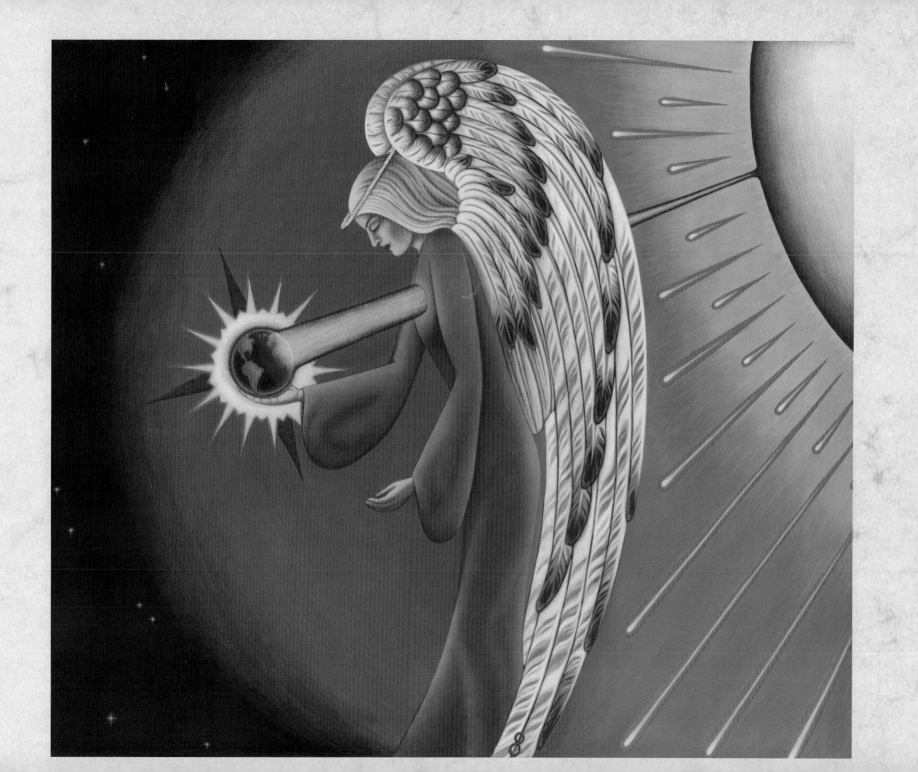

What holds it all together?
What keeps the far and near
Forever in this lovely dance
That we all hold so dear?

It's something that's within us,
Inside you and me.
It's Life and Love and Wonderous.
It's given to us free.

In this world of wonders
There are miracles galore;
Minerals, plants and animals
And people by the score.

Not one small bird's forgotten,
Not one leaf falls to ground
In which the Lord's full glory
Isn't breathtakingly found.

For shining out from under stones
And filling naked air
Lives perfect Love beyond belief
If only we're aware.

Holiness is hidden
Deep in every heart.
It's with us at the ending
And it's with us at the start.

It's worthwhile to remember
That it's in eternity
Where our enormous
selves reside
And shall forever be.

When sorrow hits us deeply,
When anger rages high
It is our souls who call to us
That one day Love shall fly.

Heaven is for real
Though sometimes hard to tell.
The angels gather close to us
And know that all is well.

One day we will remember
Who we really are
Then each and every one of us
Will shine just like a star.

Notes on my paintings

Fact Stands While Fiction Dithers

I took a course exploring the subconscious mind from the book "Journey to Freedom" by Leslie Kenton. This opened up to me a world of fascinating symbolic images. This painting is from one of those shamanic journeys, showing Ego with her Higher Self. Ego says, "I will remember God always." Higher Self says, "I do remember."

Birth of a Woman

Eclipses were seen as frightening things by ancient peoples. Leaving behind the securities of childhood can create fear in us today. But when looked upon with love – what beauty!

Contemplating the Body of God

Shamanic journey experiencing the vastness of the cosmos.

Love Cometh
Shamanic journey to life's purpose –
to pour Love upon the world, to be Love.

Shooting Stars
A painting from a photo by J. T. Nelson.
The stars are not just in the sky!

Love Cometh II
Shamanic journey – now we know where Love comes from.

Hannah Wonders
– as the universe dances across her T-shirt.

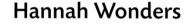

The Point
Shamanic journey – in the thin space between past and future lies The Point.
It is NOW. It is where true power lives, entwined with Love.

Easter Eggs

Jungle Pool

Seat of Joy

Shamanic journey to the place
deep inside where Joy resides.

Sweetcorn or **Golden Child**

Shadows

Physical shadows are areas where light is blocked out.
Emotional shadows are a rejection of Joy.

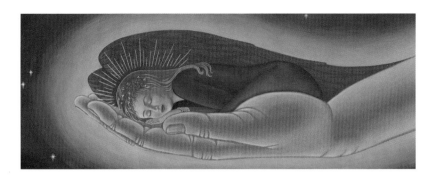

Sleeping Angel

Wise One
Shamanic journey.

Going Home

Tree of Life Exploding into Bloom
Shamanic journey.

Notes on the Music

Catherine Chandler BA (Hons)

Catherine is an accomplished musician
and (violin/viola/music) teacher with approximately 38 years
experience. She studied composition with Allan Bullard whilst at college,
and she won the Roy Teed Cup for Composition whilst in her final year.
The music written here is conceived with primary school children's voices
in mind (although, of course, this is not by any means exclusive).
The nature and subject matter of this verse is of wonderment,
and the whole composition seemed from the
first moment to be most appropriately
experienced, expressed and
enjoyed in this
way.

Patterns of Light

Verse, calligraphy and illustrations
Rebecca E Nelson

Music
Catherine Chandler

The wisdom of the heart is conveyed through symbols which speak to us on a feeling level.

It is in this felt language where awe and wonder and gratitude live.

When you go there, you find that Light is a powerful symbol of Love.

It is light that reveals to our sight the patterns of a physical life and sustains them.

It is love that reveals the patterns of inner life, and sustains them.

This book began as a song sung to my baby daughter on car journeys.

Now I would like to share with you our wonder at these beautiful patterns of light that are our universe.

In Truth we are that Light. We are that Love.

~ Rebecca